The Best of
FAVORITE RECIPES FROM QUILTERS

BREADS

Louise Stoltzfus

Good Books
Intercourse, PA 17534
Printed and bound in Hong Kong

Cover design and illustrations by Cheryl Benner
Design by Dawn J. Ranck

BREADS: THE BEST OF FAVORITE RECIPES FROM
QUILTERS
Copyright © 1994 by Good Books, Intercourse, Pennsylvania
17534
International Standard Book Number: 1-56148-111-4
Library of Congress Catalog Card Number: 94-14904

Library of Congress Cataloging-in-Publication Data

Breads / [compiled by] Louise Stoltzfus.
       p. cm. — (The Best of Favorite recipes from quilters)
    Includes index.
    ISBN 1-56148-111-4 : $7.95
    1. Bread. I. Stoltzfus, Louise, 1952- . II. Series.
TD769.B7758   1994
641.8'15—dc20   94-14904
                                            CIP

INTRODUCTION

Amid the rush and haste of life, many people seek rest and quiet in community life. Quilters find community in common goals and activities. They talk of needles and thread, fabric and stitches, and bedcovers and pieces of art. They gather in homes, fabric shops, and convention centers to share their ideas and projects.

Many quilters are also homemakers. Some treat both cooking and quilting as high art forms. Others work hard to prepare varied and healthful meals for their busy families and quilt when they have free time.

From Homemade White Bread to Sourdough Dinner Rolls to Angel Yeast Biscuits, these Bread recipes are both practical and delicious. Those who love to quilt and those who love to cook will share in the special vibrancy of this small collection.

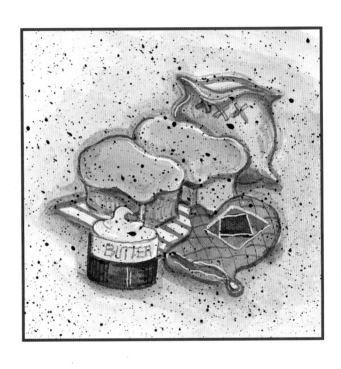

HOMEMADE WHITE BREAD

Mary Esther Yoder, Partridge, KS
Candy Horton, Greenfield, OH

1½ Tbsp. yeast
1 tsp. sugar
2 cups lukewarm water
⅓ cup cooking oil
⅓ cup white sugar
1 Tbsp. salt
5-6 cups flour

1. Sprinkle yeast and sugar into 1 cup lukewarm water. Let stand for 10 minutes.
2. Pour yeast mixture into large bowl and add all ingredients, kneading well. If dough is too sticky, add a little more flour. Place in greased bowl and cover with cloth.
3. Let rise 1 hour or until doubled in size. Punch down. Let rise again until doubled in size.
4. Form dough into 2 loaves and place into large greased loaf pans. Let rise again until nicely rounded in pans.
5. Bake at 350° on lower oven rack for 25 minutes. Remove from oven and butter tops lightly. Immediately remove bread from pans.

Makes 2 large loaves

WHOLE GRAIN BREAD

Edna Nisly, Partridge, KS

2 cups quick oatmeal
2½ cups boiling water
½ cup honey
½ cup cooking oil
2 Tbsp. salt or less
4 eggs
1 cup warm water
2 Tbsp. yeast
9½ cups whole wheat flour

1. Pour boiling water over oatmeal and let stand until cooled to lukewarm. Add honey, oil, salt and eggs. Beat one minute.
2. Dissolve yeast in warm water and add to the oatmeal mixture. Add 5 cups of flour and beat 2 minutes.
3. Add more flour and continue mixing until dough becomes too stiff for mixer. Finish mixing by hand. (Dough should be very sticky.) Turn into greased bowl, turning to grease all sides.
4. Cover and let rise until doubled in size, about 1½ hours. Knead and let rise again until doubled in size, about 45 minutes.
5. Punch down and shape into loaves. Place in greased loaf pans. Let rise again until doubled in size.
6. Bake at 350° for 35 minutes until golden brown.

Makes 3 loaves

MOM'S OATMEAL BREAD

Debra M. Zeida, Waquoit, MA

1 heaping cup oats
2 tsp. salt
½ cup molasses
4 tsp. bacon drippings or margarine
2 cups boiling water
1 yeast cake
⅓ cup warm water
5⅓ cups flour

1. Combine oats, salt, molasses and bacon drippings. Pour boiling water over mixture and let stand until cool.
2. Dissolve yeast in ⅓ cup warm water. Add to oatmeal mixture. Add flour and knead thoroughly. If dough is too sticky, add a little more flour. Place in greased bowl.
3. Let stand until doubled in size. Knead and shape into 2 loaves. Place in greased loaf pans. Let rise again until doubled in size.
4. Bake at 375° for 45 minutes. Remove from pans and grease tops with butter.

Makes 2 loaves

OATMEAL RAISIN BREAD

Susan M. Miller, Centreville, MD

½ cup warm water
2 pkgs. yeast
1¾ cups warm milk
¼ cup brown sugar, firmly packed
1 Tbsp. salt or less
3 Tbsp. margarine
5-6 cups flour
1 cup rolled oats
1 cup raisins

1. Measure warm water into large warmed bowl. Sprinkle yeast on top and stir until dissolved. Add warm milk, sugar, salt and margarine. Add 2 cups flour and beat with electric beater until smooth, about 1 minute.
2. Add 1 cup flour and oats. Beat vigorously with spoon until smooth, about 150 strokes. Add enough flour to make a soft dough. Turn out onto lightly floured board and knead until smooth and elastic, about 8-10 minutes. Cover with plastic wrap and a cloth. Let rest 20 minutes.
3. Divide dough in half and roll each into an 8" x 12" rectangle. Sprinkle ½ cup raisins over each rectangle. Shape into loaves by rolling up and tucking ends under. Place into greased loaf pans and cover loosely with plastic wrap. Let rise in warm place until doubled in size, about 1 hour.
4. Bake at 400° for 30-40 minutes or until done.

Makes 2 loaves

CREAM CHEESE BREAD

Marilyn Mowry, Irving, TX

Bread
1 cup sour cream
½ cup sugar
1 tsp. salt
½ cup margarine or butter, melted
2 pkgs. dry yeast
½ cup warm water
2 eggs
4 cups sifted flour

Cream Cheese Mixture
2 8-oz. pkgs. cream cheese
¾ cup sugar
1 egg, beaten
⅛ tsp. salt
2 tsp. vanilla

Glaze
2 cups powdered sugar
4 Tbsp. milk
2 tsp. vanilla

1. To prepare bread stir sour cream over low heat in pan. Add sugar, salt and melted margarine.
2. Sprinkle yeast over warm water in large bowl and let dissolve. Add sour cream mixture, eggs and flour and mix together. Cover tightly and refrigerate overnight.
3. Divide dough into 4 parts and roll each piece into an 8" x 12" rectangle.
4. To prepare cream cheese mixture combine all ingredients and mix until smooth. Spread ¼ of mixture onto each rectangle of dough.
5. Roll up starting with long side. Tuck under ends. Slit each roll diagonally across top (2-3 times). Arrange on greased baking sheet. Cover and let rise in warm place for 1 hour.
6. Bake at 350° for 12-15 minutes or until browned.
7. To prepare glaze combine all ingredients and mix until smooth. While loaves are still warm, cover with glaze.

Makes 4 small loaves

A group of quilters between the ages of thirty and seventy meets every Wednesday evening in my basement family room. In spite of our age differences, my husband vows he has never heard a gap in our communication. It is so wonderful to be part of the common thread of quilting.

Betty Richards, Rapid City, SD

DILLY CASSEROLE BREAD

Betty Caudle, Colorado Springs, CO

1 pkg. yeast
¼ cup warm water
1 cup cottage cheese
2 Tbsp. sugar
1 Tbsp. minced onion flakes
1 Tbsp. butter
2 Tbsp. dill seed
1 tsp. salt
¼ tsp. baking soda
1 egg
2¼-2½ cups flour

1. Soften yeast in water.
2. Heat cottage cheese to lukewarm. In a mixing bowl combine cottage cheese, sugar, onion, butter, dill seed, salt, baking soda, egg and softened yeast.
3. Add flour to form a stiff dough, beating well after each addition. Cover and let rise in warm place until light and doubled in size. Stir down.
4. Turn into well-greased 2-quart casserole dish. Let rise again.
5. Bake at 350° for 40-50 minutes. Brush top with butter and sprinkle with salt.

Makes 8-12 servings

ENGLISH MUFFIN BREAD

Maryellen Mross, Bartonsville, PA

2 pkgs. dry yeast
6 cups flour
1 Tbsp. sugar
2 tsp. salt
¼ tsp. baking soda
2 cups milk
½ cup water
Yellow cornmeal

1. Combine yeast, 3 cups flour, sugar, salt and baking soda.
2. Heat milk and water until very warm. Add to dry mixture and beat well. Add remaining 3 cups flour to make a stiff batter.
3. Grease 2 loaf pans and dust insides with cornmeal. Spoon dough into pans and sprinkle with cornmeal. Cover and let rise for 45 minutes.
4. Bake at 400° for 25-30 minutes. Cool on wire rack. Slice, toast and enjoy.

Makes 2 loaves

SOURDOUGH DINNER ROLLS

Elaine W. Good, Lititz, PA

1 cup sourdough starter
1 cup warm water (115°)
½ tsp. baking soda
½ cup cooking oil
1 egg
1 tsp. salt
¼ cup sugar
4½-5 cups white bread flour

1. Combine starter, water and baking soda in a plastic or glass bowl, stirring with a plastic or wooden spoon. Do not use metal.
2. Combine oil and egg and stir into starter mixture. Add salt and sugar.
3. Add flour, 1 or 2 cups at a time, and stir until dough cleans the bowl. Turn out onto floured surface, cover with bowl and let rest 10 minutes. Knead thoroughly.
4. Shape dough into 24 rolls and place in a greased 9" x 13" baking pan (may be metal).
5. Cover with damp cloth and let rise in a warm place for several hours. (I use my oven with the light turned on.)
6. Bake at 350° for 20 minutes.

Makes 24 rolls

Note: *I received my first starter from a friend. If you do not have Sourdough Starter, you may begin your own. (See Sourdough Starter recipe on page 16.)*

SOURDOUGH STARTER

Elaine W. Good, Lititz, PA

1 Tbsp. yeast
2 cups warm water
2 cups unbleached flour
¼ cup sugar

1. Dissolve yeast in warm water in a 2-quart glass jar, crock or plastic container. Do not use metal. Let stand 10 minutes.
2. Stir in flour and sugar. Cover and let stand at room temperature until bubbly and slightly sour smelling. This will take a day or two.
3. After measuring the amount you need for a recipe, feed your starter with 1 cup unbleached flour, 1 cup milk and ¼ cup sugar.
4. Store at room temperature, stirring it down every day and using it at least once a week.
5. If you cannot use starter, but it needs to be fed, replenish with a "half feed" occasionally. Add ½ cup flour, ½ cup milk and 2 Tbsp. sugar.
6. If the quantity does grow out of its container, simply freeze some or all of the starter. You may do this whenever you are weary of its company or if you plan to be gone for awhile.
7. Bring starter to room temperature, and it is ready to use again.

SQUASH YEAST ROLLS

Alma C. Ranck, Paradise, PA

5½-6 cups flour
⅓ cup dry milk
2 pkgs. dry yeast
½ tsp. mace
12-oz. pkg. frozen squash, cooked
1 cup water
½ cup sugar
3 Tbsp. shortening
2 tsp. salt

I have fond memories of learning to quilt as a teenager in our small Amish community. Once a month the church women got together to sew and quilt for the needy. My mother would load the buggy with a quilt frame which stuck out the front and back, a sewing machine tied to the back, a potluck dish for the noon meal and small children and bundles of supplies filling the back seat. Today I watch my grandchildren learning to quilt as our current church group continues to meet once a month.

Edna Nisly, Partridge, KS

1. Stir together 2 cups flour, dry milk, yeast and mace. Set aside.
2. In a saucepan combine squash, water, sugar, shortening and salt. Heat slowly until warm (120-130°), stirring to blend.
3. Add liquid ingredients to flour and yeast mixture. Beat until smooth, about 1 minute on medium speed or 300 strokes by hand. Beat 2 minutes at high speed.
4. Stir in remaining flour to make a moderately soft dough. Turn out onto lightly floured board and knead until smooth, about 5-10 minutes. Place in greased bowl, turning to grease all sides.
5. Cover and let rise in warm place (80-85°) until doubled in size, about 1½ hours. Punch down. Let rise again for about 10 minutes.
6. Divide dough into fourths and shape each portion into 7 rolls. Place on greased sheet pan. Cover and let rise in warm place until doubled in size, about 30 minutes.
7. Bake at 350° for 25-35 minutes or until done. Brush tops lightly with butter and cover rolls.

Makes 28 rolls

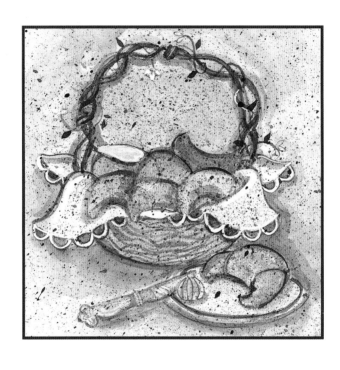

DINNER ROLLS

Lillian McAninch, Leesburg, FL

2 pkgs. dry yeast
½ cup warm water
½ cup sugar
2 eggs
1 tsp. salt
⅔ cup margarine
1 cup mashed potatoes
1 cup milk, room temperature
6½ cups flour
1-2 Tbsp. margarine, melted

1. Dissolve yeast in warm water. Set aside.
2. Beat together sugar and eggs. Add salt, margarine, potatoes, milk, yeast and 3 cups flour. Beat at least 10 strokes.
3. Add remaining flour and knead until smooth. Place in a greased bowl.
4. Let rise in warm place until almost doubled in size. Punch down.
5. Divide dough into 5 parts and roll each out into a circle. Cut into 8 wedges. Roll up each wedge, starting at wide edge. Place on greased sheet pans. Let rise again until doubled in size. Brush tops with melted margarine.
6. Bake at 375° for 10 minutes. Brush tops again with melted margarine.

Makes 40 small rolls

QUICK LIGHT ROLLS

Ella Miller, Fredericksburg, OH

1 cup milk
5 Tbsp. sugar
1 tsp. salt
1 pkg. dry yeast
1 cup lukewarm water
5 cups enriched flour
6 Tbsp. lard, melted

1. Scald milk, add sugar and salt and cool to lukewarm.
2. Dissolve yeast in warm water. Add to cooled milk mixture.
3. Sift flour. Add 2½ cups to yeast mixture, beating until smooth.
4. Add melted lard and remaining flour. Knead well and let rise until doubled in bulk, about 1½ hours. Shape into rolls, cover and let rise about 1 hour or until doubled in size. Place into greased muffin tins.
5. Bake at 350° for 15 minutes.

Makes 2 dozen rolls

ZWIEBACK

Judy Miller, Hutchinson, KS

2 cups milk
1 cup shortening
2 tsp. salt
4 Tbsp. sugar
1 yeast cake
2 tsp. sugar
1 cup lukewarm water
2 eggs, beaten (optional)
8-10 cups sifted flour

1. Scald milk. Add shortening, salt and 4 Tbsp. sugar. Cool to lukewarm.
2. Crumble yeast in a small bowl. Add 2 tsp. sugar and warm water. Put in a warm place until spongy.
3. Add yeast mixture and beaten eggs to lukewarm milk mixture. Mix well and gradually stir in flour. Knead until very soft and smooth.
4. Cover and let rise in a warm place until doubled in bulk.
5. Pinch off balls of dough about the size of a small egg, and arrange about an inch apart on a greased baking sheet. Put a similar ball, but slightly smaller, on top of each bottom ball. Press down with thumb. Let rise until doubled in bulk, about 1 hour.
6. Bake at 375-400° for 15-20 minutes.

Makes about 4 dozen Zwieback

ANGEL YEAST BISCUITS

Betty Sereno, Terra Alta, WV

1 pkg. dry yeast
½ cup warm water
5 cups flour
1 tsp. baking soda
3 tsp. baking powder
3 Tbsp. sugar
¾ cup shortening
2 cups buttermilk

1. Dissolve yeast in warm water. Set aside.
2. Sift together all dry ingredients. Cut shortening into dry mixture until well mixed. Add buttermilk and yeast and work together with a large spoon.
3. Place dough in a large, greased bowl. Cover and refrigerate until ready to use. Take out only as much dough as needed and roll to about ½-inch thickness on a floured board. Cut with a biscuit cutter.
4. Arrange on a baking sheet and let rise until doubled in size.
5. Bake at 400° for 10-15 minutes.

Makes 20 biscuits

YOGURT CRESCENT ROLLS

Carolyn Shank, Dayton, VA

⅓ cup cooking oil
8-oz. carton plain lowfat yogurt
½ cup sugar
2 pkgs. dry yeast
½ cup warm water
1 egg
1 egg white
4 cups flour
1 tsp. salt
Vegetable cooking spray

One day I attended a quilting demonstration at a local craft event. A visitor to the area (or "a tourist" as we call these people in Lancaster County) passed by, stopped and commented, "It's so nice to see all these handicapped ladies have a job." He thought each woman had only one hand! (As we all know, the other hand was under the quilt.)

Sarah S. King, Gordonville, PA

1. Combine oil, yogurt and sugar and set aside.
2. In large mixing bowl dissolve yeast in warm water. Let stand for 5 minutes.
3. Stir in yogurt mixture, egg and egg white.
4. In separate bowl combine flour and salt. Stir 2 cups flour into yogurt mixture and beat at medium speed until smooth. Gradually stir in remaining flour mixture.
5. Cover and refrigerate 8 hours or overnight. Punch dough down and divide into 4 equal parts. On a floured surface roll each into a 10-inch circle. Coat circles of dough with cooking spray. Cut each circle into 12 wedges.
6. Roll up each wedge, beginning with wide end. Arrange on greased baking sheets with point side down. Cover and let rise in warm place, free from drafts, about 45 minutes or until doubled in bulk.
7. Bake at 375° for 10-12 minutes or until golden brown.

Makes 4 dozen rolls

SOFT PRETZELS

Genny Morrow, Lancaster, PA
Esther L. Lantz, Leola, PA

1 pkg. fast-acting yeast
1½ cups warm water
¼ cup brown sugar
4-4½ cups flour
Baking soda
Kosher salt

1. In a mixing bowl combine yeast, warm water and brown sugar. Let stand for 5 minutes. Add flour and beat with a dough hook until smooth.
2. Let stand 5 minutes while you bring a deep saucepan full of water to a boil. (For every cup of water add 2 Tbsp. baking soda.)
3. Divide dough into 12 even pieces. Roll each piece into a long rope and twist into a pretzel shape.
4. Drop each pretzel into boiling water and boil for 10 seconds. Remove with a slotted spoon. Arrange pretzels on a greased baking sheet and sprinkle with kosher salt.
5. Bake at 450° about 8 minutes or until browned.

Makes 12 pretzels

OVERNIGHT SWEET ROLLS

Esther Becker, Gap, PA

4 cups flour
¼ cup sugar
1 tsp. salt
1 cup margarine
1 pkg. yeast
¼ cup very warm water
1 cup milk
2 eggs, beaten
Soft margarine
1 cup sugar
1 tsp. cinnamon
1½ cups powdered sugar
2-3 Tbsp. milk
2 tsp. grated orange rind (optional)

1. In a large bowl combine flour, ¼ cup sugar and salt. Cut 1 cup margarine into dry ingredients.
2. Sprinkle yeast into very warm water and stir until dissolved.
3. Scald 1 cup milk and cool to lukewarm. Add yeast, milk and eggs to flour mixture. Toss until well mixed. Cover tightly and refrigerate overnight.
4. Divide dough in half. Roll each half into a 12" x 18" rectangle. Spread with soft margarine.
5. Combine 1 cup sugar and cinnamon. Sprinkle over rolled out dough. Roll up and cut into 1-inch pieces. Arrange in baking dish.
6. Bake at 400° for 15 minutes.
7. Combine powdered sugar and 2-3 Tbsp. milk. Drizzle over hot rolls. If desired, sprinkle with grated orange rind. Serve.

Makes 18 servings

During the winter when I made my first Lone Star quilt, we had a blizzard and were snowed in at home one day. A friend of one of my children was visiting. I had finished putting together the diamonds of the star and was working at adding the fill in.

Each time I added a square or triangle, the young girl expressed surprise at how it all fit together. By the time I had finished, she was ecstatic with surprise and pleasure. To this day, I never put together a Lone Star without remembering that day and feeling a bit like a magician.

Esther Becker, Gap, PA

RAISED DOUGHNUTS

Alma Mullet, Walnut Creek, OH

1¼ cups milk
¼ cup shortening
1 tsp. salt
1 small cake yeast
4½-5 cups flour, sifted
¾ cup white sugar
¼ tsp. nutmeg
3 eggs, beaten

1. In a saucepan scald milk. Add shortening and salt. Remove from heat and cool to lukewarm. Add crumbled yeast and stir. Pour into a mixing bowl.
2. Gradually add 2⅔ cups flour, beating thoroughly. Place in a warm spot and let stand until full of bubbles.
3. In a separate bowl combine sugar, nutmeg and eggs. Pour into milk and yeast mixture and mix well. Add remaining flour and knead until well mixed.
4. Cover and let rise in a warm place for about 1 hour.
5. Turn out onto lightly floured board and roll out until about ½-inch thick. Cut dough with a doughnut cutter. Let rise on a board until tops are springy when touched.
6. Deep-fry in fat at 365°. Drain doughnuts in colander and lay out to cool. Dip in choice of sugar or glaze and serve.

Makes 3 dozen doughnuts

IRISH SODA BREAD

Irene Scheid, Wood Haven, NY

3 cups flour, sifted
4 tsp. baking powder
1 tsp. salt
1 cup sugar
1 cup raisins
1 cup boiling water
2 tsp. caraway seeds (optional)
1 egg
1 cup milk
3 Tbsp. shortening

1. Combine flour, baking powder, salt and sugar and mix.
2. Pour boiling water over raisins. Let stand until cool.
   Drain and pat dry.
3. Add raisins and caraway seeds to dry ingredients.
4. In another bowl mix, milk and shortening.
   Combine all ingredients, adding more milk if needed.
   Form into round loaf and place on greased baking
   sheet.
5. Bake at 350° for 1 hour or until done. Store in tightly
   closed plastic bag to prevent hardening.

Makes 1 round loaf

MAMA'S CORNBREAD

Tommie Freeman, Carrollton, GA

1 egg
2 cups buttermilk
1½ cups self-rising cornmeal
½ cup self-rising flour
1 tsp. sugar
¼ cup cooking oil

1. Break egg into 2-quart bowl and add buttermilk. Add cornmeal, flour and sugar and mix well.
2. Grease a medium iron skillet and heat it. Pour oil into cornmeal mixture and mix well. Pour mixture into hot skillet.
3. Bake at 400° for about 30 minutes or until golden brown.

Makes 6-8 servings

GRANDMA'S JOHNNY CAKE

Marie E. Fuller, Ashfield, MA

1 cup cornmeal
1 cup flour
½ cup sugar
1 tsp. cream of tartar
½ tsp. baking soda
½ tsp. salt
2 Tbsp. butter
1 cup milk
1 egg

1. Mix together all dry ingredients. Cut in butter with pastry blender or two knives until well mixed.
2. In separate bowl combine milk and egg. Add to dry ingredients and stir until just moistened. Pour into greased 9-inch square baking pan.
3. Bake at 400° for 20 minutes.

Makes 10-12 servings

ONION CHEESE CORNBREAD

Mary Lou Kirtland, Berkeley Heights, NJ

4 Tbsp. margarine
1 large Spanish onion, thinly sliced
¾ cup sour cream
1 cup shredded cheddar cheese
1 pkg. cornbread mix
8-oz. can cream-style corn
⅓ cup milk
1 egg

1. In frying pan melt margarine and sauté onion until transparent. Add sour cream and ½ cup shredded cheese and mix well.
2. In mixing bowl blend cornbread mix, cream-style corn, milk and egg. Spread into greased 9-inch square baking pan.
3. Spread onion mixture over cornbread. Sprinkle with remaining cheese.
4. Bake at 425° for 35-40 minutes. Serve hot.

Makes 8-10 servings

RITA'S DATE BREAD

M. Jeanne Osborne, Sanford, ME

1 cup sugar
½ cup margarine
½ cup sour cream
1 tsp. vanilla
3 mashed bananas
2 eggs
2 cups flour
1 tsp. baking soda
¼ tsp. salt
1 cup chopped dates
½ cup chopped raisins
½ cup chopped walnuts

1. Combine all ingredients and mix well. Pour batter into greased loaf pan.
2. Bake at 350° for 45-60 minutes.

Makes 1 loaf

BEET BREAD

Abbie Christie, Berkeley Heights, NJ

3-ozs. unsweetened chocolate
1 cup cooking oil
1¾ cups sugar
3 large eggs
2 cups puréed beets
1 tsp. vanilla
2 cups flour
2 tsp. baking soda
½ tsp. salt

1. Melt chocolate with ¼ cup oil. Cool slightly.
2. Beat sugar and eggs with mixer until light and fluffy. Slowly beat in remaining ¾ cup oil, beets, chocolate and vanilla.
3. Sift together flour, baking soda and salt. Slowly add to batter, stirring well. Spoon into greased and floured 12-cup bundt pan.
4. Bake at 375° for 1 hour. Cool 15 minutes in pan.

Makes 10-12 servings

POPPY SEED BREAD

Sue Hertzler Schrag, Beatrice, NE

Dough
3 cups flour
1½ tsp. salt
1½ tsp. baking powder
2¼ cups sugar
3 eggs
1½ cups milk
1⅛ cups cooking oil
1½ Tbsp. poppy seeds
1½ tsp. vanilla
1½ tsp. almond flavoring
1½ tsp. butter flavoring

Glaze
¾ cup sugar
¼ cup orange juice
½ tsp. vanilla
1½ tsp. almond flavoring
1½ tsp. butter flavoring

1. Combine all dough ingredients and beat 2 minutes with mixer. Spoon into 2 large greased loaf pans.
2. Bake at 350° for 1 hour or until toothpick comes out clean. Remove from oven and cool 5 minutes.
3. To prepare glaze combine all ingredients and mix well. Pour glaze over slightly cooled bread and return to oven for 10 minutes. Remove and cool 5 minutes before turning bread out of pans.

Makes 2 loaves

My grandmother, Doña Ana Wright Daugherty, was a beautiful and joyful woman who loved to quilt and cook. When I stayed with her, she occasionally would let me nap on a Victorian Crazy Quilt. I remember the feeling of deep pile velvet against my cheek and the outline of beautiful embroidery around the irregular patches of upholstery brocades, silks and velvets. The mysterious colors and textures of this rich quilt became my original inspiration when I too became a quilter.

I also cherish the memory of helping her make her famous biscuits. She always let me help even though I made a big mess of things. From her legacy I have learned to take pleasure in cooking and cleaning and sewing. Her art was her life, and her life was an art form that has greatly inspired me.

Katy J. Widger, Los Lunas, NM

PUMPKIN BANANA BREAD

Lois Stoltzfus, Honey Brook, PA

½ cup sugar
1 large banana, mashed
¾ cup cooking oil
1 cup mashed pumpkin
2 eggs
2 cups all-purpose flour
1 tsp. baking soda
½ tsp. baking powder
½ tsp. salt
2 tsp. vanilla

1. Mix sugar, banana, oil, pumpkin and eggs in large bowl. Stir in remaining ingredients until just mixed. Pour into greased loaf pan.
2. Bake at 325° for 60-70 minutes or until wooden pick inserted in center comes out clean.
3. Let cool 10 minutes. Remove from pan and cool completely before slicing.

Makes 1 loaf

LEMON BREAD

Maureen Csikasz, Wakefield, MA

Batter
½ cup shortening
1 cup sugar
2 eggs, beaten
1½ cups flour
½ tsp. salt
1 tsp. baking powder
½ cup milk
½ cup chopped nuts (optional)
Rind of 1 lemon, grated

Topping
Juice of 1 lemon
½ cup sugar

1. Cream together shortening and sugar. Add eggs and mix well.
2. Sift together flour, salt and baking powder. Add to creamed mixture, alternating with milk. Fold in nuts and lemon rind. Spoon into greased loaf pan.
3. Bake at 350° for 45-60 minutes.
4. To prepare topping combine lemon juice and sugar and mix well. After bread is baked, turn out onto plate right side up and cool about 10 minutes. Pour topping over bread. Cool completely.

Makes 8 servings

Variation: *Add ¼ tsp. almond extract to ingredients in step 1. Pour batter into 8" x 4" Corning-style baking pan. Here in the mountains I bake this recipe at 325° for 70 minutes or until toothpick comes out clean when inserted in center.*

Sue Seeley, Black Forest, CO

My mother died of cancer in 1987 after being sick for a very long time. I don't think I could have gotten through the many hours I spent at her bedside if it had not been for quilting. I look now at the quilts I made during that time (most were wall hangings so I could carry them with me), and I remember our conversations, our shared worries and our laughter. Those quilts are my link to her. Indeed, quilts are more than just coverings for beds and walls; they are living memories which join us to our past.

Mary Puskar, Baltimore, MD

ORANGE BREAD

Thelma Swody, Stonington, CT

1 cup sugar
½ cup butter
2 eggs
1 cup sour cream
Rind of 1 orange, grated
2 cups flour
1 tsp. baking soda
½ cup sugar
Juice of 1 orange

1. Cream together 1 cup sugar and butter. Add eggs, sour cream and rind of orange.
2. Sift together flour and baking soda. Mix into creamed ingredients. Spoon into 2 greased medium loaf pans.
3. Bake at 350° for 50 minutes.
4. Mix together ½ cup sugar and orange juice and pour over bread while still hot. Cool 10 minutes and invert. Enjoy!

Makes 2 loaves

RAISIN BRAN MUFFINS

Rose Fitzgerald, Delaware, OH
Connee Sager, Tucson, AZ
Susie Braun, Rapid City, SD
Lori Drohman, Rogue River, OR
Cyndie Marrara, Port Matilda, PA

4 eggs, beaten
1 quart buttermilk
5 tsp. baking soda
3 cups sugar
5 cups unsifted flour
1 cup cooking oil
15-oz. box raisin bran flakes

1. Combine all ingredients well and refrigerate at least overnight. Batter will keep as long as six weeks.
2. Spoon desired amount of batter into greased muffin tins.
3. Bake at 400° for 15 minutes.

Makes 6 dozen muffins

Variation: *Instead of raisin bran flakes pour 2 cups boiling water over 2 cups 100% bran cereal and let cool. Stir in 4 cups All-Bran and add raisins as desired. Mix with other ingredients and proceed as given.*

Ruth Liebelt, Rapid City, SD

BEST BRAN MUFFINS

Margaret M. McTigue, Scarsdale, NY

1 Tbsp. molasses
¼ cup brown sugar
½ cup butter or margarine
1 tsp. baking soda
1 cup milk
½ cup flour
2 cups bran flakes
½ cup raisins
1 egg

1. Cream together molasses, brown sugar and butter. Stir in all remaining ingredients and let stand several minutes to soften bran flakes. Mix well.
2. Spoon into greased muffin tins.
3. Bake at 400° for 15-20 minutes, watching closely to prevent burning.

Makes 12 small muffins

APPLE RAISIN MUFFINS

Susan M. Miller, Centreville, MD

¾ cup cooking oil
1 cup sugar
2 eggs
1 tsp. vanilla
2 cups flour
¾ tsp. baking soda
1 tsp. cinnamon
½ tsp. salt
1½ cups diced apples
½ cup raisins
½ cup chopped walnuts

1. In a large bowl beat oil and sugar with electric mixer for 2 minutes. Add eggs and vanilla and beat 1 minute.
2. In separate bowl stir together flour, baking soda, cinnamon and salt. Add to creamed mixture and stir until just moist. Fold in apples, raisins and walnuts. Fill 12 greased muffin cups ¾ full.
3. Bake at 400° for 25-30 minutes or until done. Remove from pan and cool on rack. May be served warm or cold.

Makes 12 muffins

SPICY WHOLE WHEAT ZUCCHINI MUFFINS

Sue Gierhart, Voorhees, NJ

1 cup whole wheat flour
¾ cup unbleached white flour
¼ cup wheat germ
¼ cup sugar
1 Tbsp. baking powder
¼ tsp. baking soda
½ tsp. cinnamon
¼ tsp. allspice
Dash salt
1 cup milk
1 egg, lightly beaten
¼ cup cooking oil
1 cup grated, unpeeled zucchini
⅓ cup raisins

1. In mixing bowl combine flours, wheat germ, sugar, baking powder, baking soda, spices and salt.
2. Pour milk into 2-cup (or larger) measuring cup. Add egg and oil and blend well.
3. Pour milk mixture over dry ingredients and add zucchini and raisins. Stir just enough to moisten. Do not over-mix.
4. Spoon batter into greased muffin cups.
5. Bake at 400° for 20-22 minutes.

Makes 12 muffins

CRANBERRY ORANGE MUFFINS

Susan Harms, Wichita, KS

1 cup fresh cranberries, chopped
½ cup sugar
1 tsp. grated orange peel
1¾ cups all-purpose flour
2½ tsp. baking powder
¾ tsp. salt
1 egg, beaten
¼ cup orange juice
½ cup milk
⅓ cup cooking oil

1. Mix cranberries, sugar and orange peel. Set aside.
2. Sift together flour, baking powder and salt in large bowl.
3. In separate bowl combine egg, orange juice, milk and cooking oil. Add to dry ingredients, stirring until just moistened. Fold in cranberry mixture. Fill 12 greased muffin cups ⅔ full.
4. Bake at 400° for 20-25 minutes. Serve warm.

Makes 12 muffins

WHOLE WHEAT OAT BLUEBERRY MUFFINS

Betty Ann Sheganoski, Bayonne, NJ

2 eggs
3 Tbsp. sunflower oil
½ cup honey
¾ cup buttermilk
¾ tsp. vanilla
¾ cup oats
1¾ cups whole wheat flour
1⅓ tsp. baking soda
1⅓ tsp. baking powder
1 tsp. cinnamon
1¾ cups blueberries

1. Combine eggs, oil, honey, buttermilk, vanilla and oats and soak for 10 minutes.
2. In a separate bowl combine all dry ingredients. Pour dry ingredients into wet ingredients and mix well. Fold in blueberries. Spoon into greased muffin tins.
3. Bake at 375° for 18-20 minutes.

Makes 12 muffins

LEMON NUT MUFFINS

Trudi Cook, Newtown Square, PA

Batter
1¾ cups flour
1 cup chopped walnuts
⅓ cup sugar
2 tsp. baking powder
1 tsp. grated lemon rind
½ tsp. salt
1 egg
½ cup milk
⅓ cup butter or margarine, melted
¼ cup sour cream

Streusel Topping
3 Tbsp. flour
3 Tbsp. brown sugar
3 Tbsp. wheat germ
2 Tbsp. softened butter or margarine
1 tsp. grated lemon rind

1. To prepare batter combine flour, walnuts, sugar, baking powder, lemon rind and salt in large bowl.
2. In a small bowl beat egg with fork. Stir in milk, butter and sour cream. Add to flour mixture, stirring until just blended.
3. To prepare streusel topping combine all ingredients and mix until crumbly.
4. Fill greased muffin tins ⅔ full with batter. Sprinkle with streusel topping.
5. Bake at 400° for 15-20 minutes or until toothpick inserted in center comes out clean.

Makes 12 muffins

During Easter vacation I received an anguished call from my daughter. She was so upset; I was sure something had happened to one of her family. When she was finally able to talk, she told me what had happened. Her daughter had volunteered to take care of the class bunny over school vacation. Fearing the bunny might get cold, Lindsey covered his cage with her special carrousel quilt. The next morning the family discovered, to their dismay, that Bunny had liked the quilt so much that he ate big chunks of it by pulling it into the cage. My daughter was sure she would be severely reprimanded by me. I was so grateful that all her family members were alive and healthy that I reminded her, "Yes, a quilt is a treasured possession, but it is still a thing—not a being—and it may be repaired or replaced." Today Lindsey's repaired carrousel quilt includes a label which tells the story of Peter Rabbit's Easter breakfast.

M. Jeanne Osborne, Sanford, ME

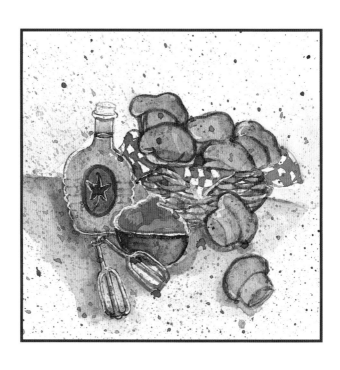

SWEET POTATO MUFFINS

Teresa M. Prete, East Falmouth, MA

¾ cup flour
1½ tsp. baking powder
½ tsp. cinnamon
Dash nutmeg
6 ozs. cooked and peeled sweet potato, mashed
½ cup maple syrup
1 egg, beaten
2 Tbsp. cooking oil

1. In medium bowl combine flour, baking powder, cinnamon and nutmeg.
2. In small bowl combine remaining ingredients, mixing until egg is thoroughly combined. Stir into dry ingredients until just moistened. Spoon batter into 6 greased muffin cups.
3. Bake at 400° for 20-25 minutes. Cool muffins on wire rack.

Makes 6 muffins

SAVORY CHEESE MUFFINS

Florence Heard, St. Marys, ON

2 cups all-purpose flour
2 Tbsp. baking powder
½ tsp. salt
½ cup softened butter
¼ cup sugar
2 eggs
1 cup milk
1 cup grated cheddar cheese
1 tsp. basil

1. Sift together flour, baking powder and salt.
2. Cream together butter and sugar. Add eggs and beat
   well. Gradually add dry ingredients, alternating with
   milk. Quickly fold in cheese and basil. Spoon into
   greased muffin tins.
3. Bake at 350° for 25-30 minutes.

Makes 12 muffins

Southern Gal Biscuits

Donna Miller, Partridge, KS

2 cups flour
4 tsp. baking powder
½ tsp. salt
2 Tbsp. sugar
½ tsp. cream of tartar
½ cup shortening
¾ cup milk
1 egg

1. Sift together flour, baking powder, salt, sugar and cream of tartar. Add shortening and mix well. Add milk and egg. Stir to make stiff dough.
2. Roll out to 1-inch thickness. Cut biscuits with cookie cutter and arrange on greased baking sheet.
3. Bake at 450° for 10-15 minutes.

Makes 6 biscuits

INDEX